THE RID
THE STONES
and other Unsolved Mysteries

THE RIDDLE OF THE STONES
and other Unsolved Mysteries

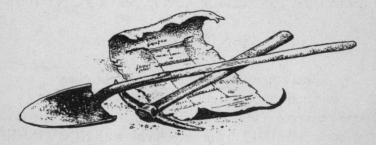

DANIEL COHEN
ILLUSTRATED BY PETER DENNIS

SCHOLASTIC INC.
New York Toronto London Auckland Sydney

ISBN 0-590-93713-8

Text copyright © 1995 by Daniel Cohen.
Illustrations copyright © 1995 by Peter Dennis.
All rights reserved. Published by Scholastic Inc., 555 Broadway, New York, NY 10012, by arrangement with KINGFISHER, Larousse Kingfisher Chambers Inc.

12 11 10 9 8 7 6 5 4 3 2   6 7 8 9/9 0 1 2/0

Printed in the U.S.A.
First Scholastic printing, September 1996

❖ Contents ❖

OUR UNKNOWN WORLD

Planes and ships that suddenly vanish; people who suddenly appear or who disappear; things that are seen in the sky, or things that strike the earth with a devastating impact. These are some of the unsolved mysteries that you will read about in the pages that follow. They are the sort of events that will make you wonder if things really are what they seem....

✤ *Sudden Impact* ✤

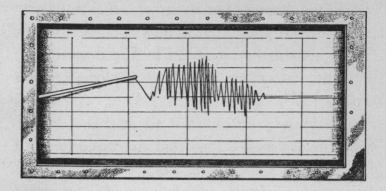

I magine the eerie silence of a remote forest in Siberia. Now imagine what an explosion with the force of a nuclear bomb would sound like there. Just such a blast thundered across the dark, wooded Siberian plains at exactly 7:17 A.M. on June 30, 1908. Villagers living 40 miles away saw a bluish white streak cut across the sky followed by "a pillar of fire" and monstrous clouds of black smoke. Thinking it was the Day of Judgment predicted in the Bible, they fell on their knees in prayer. Nearly 750 miles away, the Trans-Siberian Express was derailed by the shock wave from the impact.

Seismographs—the scientific instruments that measure earthquakes—indicated that an earthquake had taken place in the Tunguska region of Siberia, an area where earthquakes are virtually unknown. For months, the entire world experienced spectacular dawns and sunsets. These are usually produced by the dust thrown into the atmosphere by a huge explosion, like a volcano.

Amazingly, no one put all of this together. Siberian newspapers reported the explosion, but these reports were not read beyond Siberia itself. Scientists in other parts of the world speculated about the seismographic readings and the strange weather. But that was all.

Conditions in Russia at the time were so chaotic, and the area of the explosion was so remote, that it wasn't until 1927—nearly twenty years later—that a scientific expedition actually visited the site. The expedition, headed by Leonid Kulik, had pieced together enough information to come up with the theory that the explosion had been caused by a giant meteorite that had fallen from the sky. Kulik expected to find a crater, or hole in the earth, dug by the meteorite after it fell.

As Kulik approached the site he found mile after mile of trees that had been burned and flattened by the blast. All the fallen trees pointed away from the center of the explosion. But at the center where Kulik assumed the crater would be, there was nothing. In fact, at the very center a few stripped and burned trees were still standing.

Kulik made three additional expeditions to the area, and until the day he died he remained convinced that the cause had been a giant meteorite. But without a crater or meteorite fragment to prove it, the Great Siberian Explosion remains a mystery.

Over the years, many other theories have been suggested. One explanation was that a piece of comet had either hit the earth or, more likely, exploded above the surface. Comets are made up of frozen gases that have small solid particles embedded in them. Other scientists suggested that a piece of antimatter or part of a black hole struck Siberia. One bizarre idea was that a nuclear-powered spaceship from another planet had exploded over the area.

Finally, in 1992 a scientific team that had been studying the puzzle for years announced that the blast had been caused by a stony asteroid, some 3,000 yards in diameter, which had exploded five miles above the earth's surface. Because the explosion had been in the air, the team argued, there was no crater. The puzzle was solved. Or was it? Some people are still not convinced.

Whatever the object was, it just happened to strike one of the most sparsely populated regions of this planet. As far as we know, not a single human death was caused by the explosion. But with a slight change of direction or angle the impact could have been in St. Petersburg or London or New York. In some ways, June 30, 1908 was a very lucky day.

❖ *Without a Trace* ❖

On the evening of November 3, 1872 two old seafaring friends, David Reed Morehouse, captain of the British ship *Dei Gratia*, and Benjamin Spooner Briggs, captain of the American ship *Mary Celeste*, had dinner together in New York. In the nearby port both their ships were being loaded with cargoes for their next transatlantic voyages.

On November 5 the *Mary Celeste* set sail for Genoa, Italy, carrying a cargo of commercial alcohol. On board were Captain Briggs, a crew of seven, Briggs's wife Sarah, and his two-year-old daughter. On November 11 the *Dei Gratia* began her journey to Gibraltar.

You can imagine Captain Morehouse's

surprise when, exactly one month later, he sighted the *Mary Celeste* abandoned and drifting off the coast of Portugal. The ship's sails were tattered and she had taken on a good deal of water, but otherwise the *Mary Celeste* seemed undamaged.

At once Morehouse sent a party of men to inspect his friend's ship. He feared the worst. But the mystery deepened with his men's reports.

The lifeboat and some navigation instruments were missing, which showed that those aboard had abandoned ship. But there was no obvious reason why they should have done so. There was plenty of food and water aboard. The departure must have been a hurried one, for most of the crew's gear, including the sailors' pipes and tobacco, had been left behind. Also left behind was the ship's log. The final entry, which reported nothing unusual, recorded the position at "about 110 miles due west of the island of Santa Maria in the Azores." If the *Mary Celeste* had been abandoned shortly after the entry was made, she must have been empty for more than a week and have drifted more than 600 miles.

Three members of the *Dei Gratia*'s crew sailed the *Mary Celeste* to Gibraltar with the *Dei*

Gratia herself close behind. They expected a friendly welcome because they had rescued the ship. But instead they found themselves under arrest. Because Captain Morehouse could have claimed a substantial sum for salvaging an abandoned ship, people suspected that he had

something to do with the disappearance of the *Mary Celeste* crew. But no evidence against Morehouse was ever produced.

A court of inquiry was set up in Gibraltar. After months of going over every scrap of available information and considering every possible theory, the court concluded that it was unable to come up with a solution to the mystery.

Outside the court, most people thought that the most likely theory was that the crew had mutinied, killed the captain and his family, then fearing punishment for their crime abandoned ship. But would the mutineers have left behind their personal things? Besides, there were no signs of struggle on the *Mary Celeste*. Could the real reason for the disappearances be far stranger?

The mystery was all the more gripping at the time because of rumors that the *Mary Celeste* was a "jinx" ship. She had been originally registered as the *Amazon*. The captain died within forty-eight hours of taking charge. On her first voyage she was seriously damaged. While being repaired she caught fire. There was a string of other disasters, until she was finally sold and later renamed *Mary Celeste*.

The ship came to a sad and violent end.

She was deliberately run aground on a reef in the West Indies, and finally went up in flames, so her owner could claim the insurance money.

The mystery of the *Mary Celeste* has fascinated people for well over a century. Many solutions, including freak waves and tornadoes, even encounters with sea monsters, have been proposed.

The most probable explanation is a simple one. Captain Briggs had never carried commercial alcohol before. He might not have been aware that in warm weather vapor can build up in alcohol barrels, causing them to explode. Two or three of the barrels in the *Mary Celeste*'s hold were found without their tops, as if this had indeed happened.

The explosions would have been fairly harmless. But Captain Briggs, fearing that his whole ship was about to blow up, may have ordered everyone into the lifeboat. If the wind had picked up, the *Mary Celeste* could have been blown away from the lifeboat or the little boat could have been swamped by a wave.

It's a reasonable explanation that fits the known facts. But there is no way of proving it, and there never will be.

People have reported seeing strange and unexplainable things in the sky since time began. In the 1890s, for example, there were reports all across America of a "mysterious airship" at a time when airships had not yet been invented. During World War II, combat pilots told of the strange glowing objects they called "foo fighters" which trailed their planes.

But why was it that in 1947 more people than ever began seriously to ask the question, "Is it possible that we are being visited by spaceships from another world?"

On June 24, 1947 Kenneth Arnold, an American pilot, was flying his single-engine plane over the Cascade mountains in western Washington

State when he saw nine brightly illuminated objects flying in formation. Though he was an experienced pilot he had never seen anything like these objects before. He described them as "flat like a pie pan and so shiny they reflected the sun like a mirror." They moved through the air "like a saucer would if you skipped it across the water."

Several perfectly natural explanations for the incident have been suggested. But when Arnold told his story to a reporter, it was picked up by newspapers and radio stations all over the world. The objects were first called flying disks, then flying saucers, and finally Unidentified Flying Objects or UFOs. Many people were completely convinced that these objects really were spaceships from another world.

Within months, hundreds of flying saucer or UFO reports were coming in from all over the

United States, indeed from all over the world. There was a rumor that in July 1947 a flying saucer had crashed in New Mexico and that the wreckage and the remains of the alien crew had been hidden by the US Air Force. In 1948 a pilot in Kentucky was killed chasing what he thought was a UFO. In 1952 jet fighters were sent up on two different days to find the UFOs that were detected on radar at Washington National Airport. The jets found nothing, but the incidents caused massive delays and confusion at the airport, and added to the "UFO fever" that was spreading across the country.

There were investigations by the government, Central Intelligence Agency (CIA) investigations, Air Force investigations, investigations by universities and individual scientists, and, of course, investigations by the hundreds of UFO groups run by ordinary people that sprang up all over America.

However, the fact remains that in nearly fifty years since the Arnold sighting of 1947, no conclusive proof of visits by extraterrestrial spaceships has ever been produced. There have been no bodies of little people from crashed spacecraft, no pieces of spaceship, not even a page from an alien "captain's log"—in short, not a single piece of clear physical evidence.

The United States government was somewhat secretive about its early UFO investigations. It's important to remember that this was during the Cold War between the U.S.A. and what was then the Soviet Union. At first the government was afraid that the UFOs might actually be Soviet secret weapons.

There have been plenty of photographs, even films, of what appear to be spaceships. In most cases these photos and films have been shown to be either deliberate hoaxes or misidentifications of clouds, aircraft, or other ordinary objects. Yet there are a few photos that remain unidentified, and so genuinely mysterious.

Most of the evidence for UFOs rests on reports—hundreds of thousands of them—by ordinary people who have seen what they genuinely believe to be a strange and unearthly craft in the sky. As with the pictures, there have been hoaxes and many, many mistaken identifications. The planet Venus, for example, often causes great excitement when it is seen glowing in the sky. Experienced pilots, even astronomers, have made mistakes. But there are some accounts which are puzzling and hard to explain away as sightings of familiar objects.

Surveys of public opinion have shown that a majority of people in America believe that UFOs are real and that beings from outer space do visit our planet.

Whatever Kenneth Arnold saw back in June 1947, he certainly started something, and it isn't over yet.

❖ *Alien Abductions* ❖

On the night of September 19, 1961 Betty and Barney Hill of Portsmouth, New Hampshire, were driving home from a vacation in Niagara Falls. It was late, shortly before midnight, when they saw a bright object moving in the sky. The object seemed to be following them. The road was deserted and nobody lived in the area. There were no other witnesses to what may have happened. After a while, the object appeared to land in front of them. It seemed to be some sort of disklike craft, and at the windows they could see figures wearing shiny black uniforms and black caps.

Some two-and-a-half hours later and many miles from where they first saw the UFO, the

Hills were back on the road driving home. They had no conscious recollection of what had happened to them. But the experience left them both with feelings of extreme anxiety and horrible nightmares.

They finally went to a psychiatrist, Dr. Benjamin Simon, who hypnotized them. Under hypnosis the Hills recalled being captured by alien creatures from the UFO, taken aboard the craft, and subjected to a humiliating physical examination. They were then returned to their car with all conscious memory of the experience having been erased from their minds.

At first it appeared as if the Hills' experience (which was later the subject of a bestselling book) was both bizarre and unique. But very soon others began to report similar experiences. On October 11, 1973 Calvin Parker and Charles Hickson said that they were briefly abducted by the crew of a UFO while fishing in the river near Pascagoula, Mississippi. Travis Walton, a young woodcutter working in the Apache-Sitgreaves National Forest in Arizona, claimed that he was abducted on November 5, 1975 and held for five days before being released. He said that he was able to remember very little of what happened to him during the time he was missing.

In 1986 author Whitley Streiber wrote an enormously successful book called *Communion* which tells of his abduction by space aliens. Streiber's account is a very complex and detailed one. He claimed that he had been kidnapped for a short time from his country home in New York State at Christmastime in 1985. But Streiber didn't stop there. He said that this abduction had been just one event in a long series of encounters with extraterrestrials that had begun when he was a child. His memory of all of these events was fuzzy and incomplete until he was hypnotized and was able to "recover" his memories.

These are just a few of the best-known alien abduction reports. There are hundreds like them that have come from all over the world. But are they real mysteries waiting to be solved or just inventions of the imagination?

In 1994 Dr. John E. Mack, a well-known professor of psychiatry from Harvard University, wrote a book in which he described interviews that he had conducted with people who said that they had been abducted by aliens. The doctor believed what he was told and his book convinced many people who had doubted the

abduction stories.

Even so, one of the big problems with most abduction accounts is that they are recalled only under hypnosis, and hypnotized people do not always tell the truth. They may tell what they *believe* to be the truth, but they sometimes make up elaborate fantasies about events that never happened.

Even among those who sincerely believe in UFOs, who believe that the earth is being visited by spaceships from other planets, the idea that it's possible for someone to be driving down the road, or simply be asleep at home, then suddenly be snatched up by extraterrestrial kidnappers and have all memory of the incident erased from their mind can seem far-fetched. But people like Betty and Barney Hill were sure that this was exactly what had happened to them.

Even though there is no physical evidence that any encounters with alien beings have ever taken place, the stories are fascinating and disturbing. And new stories of such experiences continue to be told.

The Riddle of
❖ *the Stones* ❖

Stonehenge... The very word conjures up images of white-robed Druids, the priests of the ancient Celts, conducting dreadful human sacrifices among the gigantic stones of the famous monument.

The image is a completely false one. Stonehenge was built long before the Druids existed. The Druids didn't build it and they probably didn't even use it.

There is no great mystery about who created Stonehenge. It was built by the people who lived in and around what is now Salisbury Plain in England. Construction began nearly 5,000 years ago with the digging of a large circular ditch and a six-foot-high bank piled alongside it. Over the

next fifteen hundred years or so work continued at the site. The circle of huge upright stones, topped by other huge stones called lintels, which we all think of as the *real* Stonehenge, was built around 4,000 years ago.

Cutting, shaping, and lifting the stones was an enormous task. Some of the stones were carried by rafts on rivers and then dragged over land, from as far away as Wales—at least 100 miles from the site. The people, or to be more accurate, series of different peoples who worked on Stonehenge possessed only primitive tools. But, even so, there is no real mystery about how Stonehenge was built. It took time and was backbreaking work. The monument must have

meant a great deal to those who built it.

And that is the mystery of Stonehenge. What did it mean to its builders? What was it used for?

Most Stonehenge experts believe that it was used as a temple—a place where religious ceremonies were conducted. Since no one knows anything about the religious beliefs or rites of the ancient builders, we can only guess what sort of ceremonies were once held there. Most people think that they probably had something to do with the movement of the Sun, the Moon, and the stars.

For a long time, those who have studied Stonehenge have known that if you stand directly in the center of the circle on the Summer Solstice, the longest day of the year, and look down an opening in the circle called The Avenue, you will see the Sun rise directly over a very distinctive standing stone called the Heel Stone.

In 1963 a British astronomer, Gerald Hawkins, suggested that there were all sorts of other possible astronomical alignments at Stonehenge. These would have been useful in determining the length of the year, and even when eclipses were to occur. Hawkins's ideas got a lot of attention. Stonehenge was called an "ancient observatory," even an "ancient computer." But historians and archaeologists who have spent their lives studying the monument are not convinced.

By about 1100 B.C., nearly 2,000 years after the first ditch was dug at Stonehenge, work on the monument stopped. By the time the Romans conquered Britain, around 2,000 years ago, Stonehenge must have been abandoned. The Romans certainly never mention it in their records, though they must have seen it. It was a place of no importance to them.

It wasn't until the 17th century that the people of Britain began to take an interest in the ancient monument. No one was even sure where the name Stonehenge came from or what it meant. There are many other stone circles or similar monuments scattered throughout the British Isles, indeed throughout Europe. But Stonehenge is by far the most famous.

There were all sorts of theories about the construction of Stonehenge. Some said it was built by giants. Others believed it had been built by Merlin the Magician as a monument to King Arthur's knights. The Romans, the Danes, and of course the Druids have all been suggested as builders of the stones.

The Druid theory became so popular that every year at the Summer Solstice, a group of people who call themselves Druids dress up in white robes and perform ancient ceremonies at Stonehenge.

But we are still no closer to knowing the real reason for the stones. We can only repeat what one observer wrote more than two hundred years ago:

"God knows what their use was."

✤ *Lost Lands* ✤

I t was an island of "marvelous beauty" in the middle of the Atlantic Ocean, with a shrine surrounded by a wall of gold, and a royal palace served by warm and cold springs. Pure fantasy? Perhaps, but in ancient Greece, somewhere around 335 B.C., the philosopher Plato wrote about a place called Atlantis that had all these things. It was a continent, Plato said, that had contained a great civilization, but the people had become so selfish and arrogant that the gods destroyed them and their land. The continent sank under the sea.

Plato's story set off one of the longest-running searches in history. Plato said he had heard the story from one of his relatives, who heard it from an Egyptian priest. There is no other mention of Atlantis in Greek or Egyptian records. Plato often made up stories to illustrate philosophical or moral ideas. For centuries, Plato's story was regarded as just that, a story.

Yet Plato's influence and reputation was so great that the Atlantis story was never forgotten. When America was reached by European explorers, some people thought it was actually Atlantis. There are a few old maps in which America is called Atlantis.

It soon became pretty clear to everyone that the New World was not Plato's Atlantis, but the discovery rekindled the idea that Atlantis existed. The hunt was on!

Ignatius Donnelly, an eccentric 19th-century American politician and scholar, wrote a book that created much excitement. In it he claimed that Atlantis was the original home of all civilization. Some people believed that Atlantis was in fact Britain; others insisted that they had found the lost continent off the island of Bermuda.

Some people wondered if Atlantis would one day rise up from the depths of the ocean. The American psychic Edgar Cayce predicted

Atlantis would reappear by the end of the 1960s, and that it would trigger a series of worldwide catastrophes. Cayce's words created panic among his followers. Of course, Atlantis didn't rise, there were no catastrophes, and the prediction was forgotten. But Atlantis was not.

Geologists and oceanographers got into the argument and pointed out that there is no evidence that there has ever been a mid-Atlantic continent. Given what we now know about the way the earth was formed, such a continent would have been impossible, they said.

Many scholars believe that Plato got the idea for his Atlantis story from garbled accounts of another ancient catastrophe. Sometime around

1400 B.C. there was a huge volcanic explosion on the island of Thera in the Aegean Sea, not far from Greece. Part of the island sank as a result. Tidal waves and falls of volcanic ash resulting from the massive explosion caused widespread destruction throughout the region.

This theory became extremely popular during the 1980s, but it did not convince everyone and it did not end the hunt for Atlantis. In 1992 a scholar named Eberhard Zangger published an influential book claiming that the origin of the Atlantis legend can be traced to an ancient Egyptian account of the Trojan War.

Atlantis isn't the only sunken continent people have searched for. There is a theory that if there is a lost continent in the middle of the Atlantic, there must also be a lost continent in the middle of the Pacific.

As with the Atlantic continent, geologists and oceanographers insist that there never was and never could be a sunken Pacific continent. But the speculation and the search for these "lost lands" continues.

✤ The Boy ✤ from Nowhere

On May 26, 1828 a boy of about seventeen limped into Unschlitt Square in Nuremberg, Germany. He was mumbling in a confused way as he stopped a passerby and handed him a letter. The boy was taken to the police station where another letter was found in his pocket. He carried no other identification.

One letter was dated October 1812, and was supposedly written by the boy's mother to someone who was to take care of him. It said the boy's father was a soldier, but had died. When the boy was seventeen he was to be sent to Nuremberg to join the army. The second letter was from a "poor laborer" who said that he and his wife had raised the boy in secret and were now sending him to join the army. It said he knew nothing of his past. The letters, however, were forgeries. They were both quite recent and written by the same person.

The boy was able to write his name, "Kaspar Hauser," but seemed unable to speak more than a few words. He spent most of his time staring at the wall. People were intrigued by the boy's strange response to certain things: he hated the sight of food, preferred darkness to light, and moved around his cell in the police station like a cat. He became a public celebrity, and hundreds flocked to see him in his cell. At first he was thought to be feeble-minded, but he quickly learned enough German to be able to communicate very well. When he spoke of his former life the mystery only deepened. He said that for as long as he could remember, he had been kept in a tiny dark dungeon where he had been unable to stand up straight and had been given only bread and water to keep him alive. One day he was given some bitter-tasting liquid to drink and when he awoke he was on the road to Nuremberg.

Kaspar's story captured the imagination of everyone, and all over Europe people argued about who he really was. Rumors began that

Kaspar was the illegitimate son of some important person, and leaflets were sent out all over Germany, but no one could throw any light on the boy's identity.

For a while Kaspar Hauser thoroughly enjoyed the attention. But as the months passed, and no further information about him was revealed, interest faded. Then in October 1829 Kaspar was found unconscious and bleeding in the cellar of the house in which he was staying. He said that he had been hit with a club by an unknown person. The mysterious attack rekindled interest in the riddle of Kaspar Hauser's true identity.

An eccentric, wealthy Englishman, Lord Charles Stanhope, took a special interest in Kaspar. He became Kaspar's guardian and moved him from Nuremberg to the town of Ansbach in

Bavaria. Here Kaspar again became the center of attention. On December 14, 1833 he staggered into his house bleeding heavily from a stab wound in his chest. He said that he had been told to go to the park and there he had been attacked by a tall man in a black cloak; he also said something about a purse.

The police found a silk purse in the park. It contained a garbled note saying that the attacker's name was "M.L.O." But nothing else could be made of the message. One curious fact emerged. It had snowed on the day of the alleged attack, and in the park there was only one set of footprints: Kaspar's own.

Kaspar Hauser's wound was more serious than it had looked, and he died three days later. His final words were, "I didn't do it to myself."

Most people who have studied the case think that Kaspar did do it to himself. They believe Kaspar staged both attacks when people stopped paying attention to him, although he probably did not mean to kill himself.

He was buried under a stone which reads in part: "Here Lies Kaspar Hauser, Riddle of Our Time." To this day no one knows who he really was or where he came from.

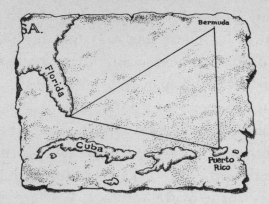

At 3:45 in the afternoon of December 5, 1945 the control tower at Fort Lauderdale, Florida, received a message from Charles Taylor, flight leader of Flight 19, a routine patrol of five Avenger torpedo-bombers.

"This is an emergency. We seem to be off course. We cannot see land... repeat... we cannot see land."

"What is your position?"

"We're not sure of our position. We can't be sure where we are. We seem to be lost."

"Head due west."

"We don't know which way is west. Everything is wrong... strange. We can't be sure of any direction. Even the ocean doesn't look as it should."

There were more messages, but they became garbled because of interference. At one point Taylor seemed to hand over control of the flight to someone else. It was clear that soon the planes would run out of fuel and might be forced to ditch at sea. At 6:27 a giant Martin Mariner flying boat, with a crew of thirteen, took off on a rescue mission. Twenty-three minutes later the Martin Mariner exploded in midair.

Pieces of the wreckage of the Martin Mariner were discovered. No trace was ever found of the planes of Flight 19. Nor did an official investigation ever find a reason for the disappearance.

The strange fate of the five Avengers was one key event in the story of the Bermuda Triangle, a triangular patch of sea with the east coast of Florida as one point of the triangle, Puerto Rico as another, and the island of Bermuda as the third. Then there was another mysterious disappearance. Early in 1963 a large tanker called the *Marine Sulphur Queen* vanished for unknown reasons, without ever sending out a distress call. A few lifejackets and pieces of debris were found, but nothing more.

It was the *Marine Sulphur Queen*'s disappearance that prompted a writer by the name of Vincent Gaddes to publish an article about all the mysterious disappearances that had taken place in that area of ocean. It was Gaddes who coined the term Bermuda Triangle. Later he also used the phrase Devil's Triangle—but Bermuda Triangle is the one that stuck.

Among the many other disappearances in the Bermuda Triangle was the *Cyclops*, which was sailing from Barbados to Norfolk, Virginia, in March 1918. It vanished with its crew of 309 without sending out a distress call and without the slightest scrap of wreckage ever being found.

Perhaps the spookiest story associated with

the Bermuda Triangle is that of the *Carroll A. Deering*. The five-masted schooner was found beached and abandoned near Cape Hatteras, North Carolina, on January 30, 1921. There wasn't a single clue as to what happened to the crew. Though Cape Hatteras is not in the Triangle, the ship sailed through the area, and many believe that the crew vanished there.

Ships and planes do vanish for mysterious, or at least unknown, reasons all over the world. The arca of the Bermuda Triangle contains some of the most heavily traveled air and sea lanes in the world. Ships and planes pass through the Triangle all the time without vanishing and without experiencing anything unusual. But many people are convinced that an abnormally high percentage of disappearances, beyond the laws of chance, do take place in the area.

There have also been reports of the navigational instruments of ships and planes passing through the region going wildly off the scale and failing to function correctly. The crew of one ship that suffered unexplained mechanical failure said it was "as if there were an invisible force field attempting to tear the ship apart."

During the 1970s the Bermuda Triangle became one of the most widely discussed mysteries ever, and dozens of books on the subject appeared. These days, many experts believe that the mystery of the Bermuda Triangle has been highly exaggerated and that most cases given as examples of its strange power are due to weather, human error, or mechanical failure.

All we can say for certain is that some disappearances, including that of Flight 19, remain unexplained.

The Oak Island
✤ *Mystery* ✤

There is a spot on little Oak Island off the coast of Nova Scotia where a fabulous treasure is supposed to be buried. The place is known as the Money Pit. It's called that not because of the treasure but because of the vast sums of money that have been poured into searching for it.

In the summer of 1795 a sixteen-year-old Nova Scotia farm boy, Daniel McGinnis, rowed out to Oak Island, which was uninhabited, to do some exploring. He found a large, old oak tree. Beneath it was a round dent in the earth. It looked as if someone had once dug a hole there, then filled it up again. Daniel felt excited. Captain Kidd, the famous pirate, was rumored to have buried some treasure somewhere off the coast of Nova Scotia. Could this be the very spot where it was hidden?

The next day Daniel returned with two friends and they began digging in the hard and heavy clay soil. It was backbreaking work. Just under the surface was a layer of flagstones which covered the circular, clay-filled pit. Ten feet down the boys found a platform of oak logs. They levered the logs out of the hole, convinced that the treasure lay just beneath. But under the logs was more clay, and after digging another ten feet there was another platform of logs. At a depth of thirty feet there was another. Exhausted and frustrated, the three boys gave up and went home. But stories of what they found began to circulate widely and attracted a stream of hopeful treasure seekers. Daniel McGinnis spent many more years in search of the treasure—to no avail.

Later, engineers with heavy machines such as diggers, some equipped with drills, were constantly frustrated by the fact that the hole they dug would fill up with water. It was years before anyone could figure out why. Then it was discovered that the main pit was connected to the seashore by an elaborate series of drains.

They were cleverly designed to flood the pit with seawater whenever any diggers got below a certain level.

One treasure-hunting expedition sank a drill into the pit that brought up samples of whatever it drilled through. It encountered what appeared to be two wooden chests filled with metal pieces—but the only metallic things brought up were "three links resembling the links of an ancient watch chain." The drill did bring up pieces of coconut fiber—there are no coconuts growing within 1200 miles of Oak Island—and putty of the type that was once used on wooden ships. Unfortunately, when the drillers tried to sink another shaft, water had already filled the pit and the chests could no longer be found.

Expedition after expedition tried different methods of getting to the treasure. Unsuccessful attempts have been made to dam up the tunnels which flood the hole. In 1971 a TV camera was lowered 260 feet into the pit and it caught an image of what may have been a severed human hand, well preserved by the sea water. The hand has not been found since.

All the digging and flooding has so weakened the area that a large section of ground around the pit has collapsed, creating a massive crater. Whatever is in the pit must have been shifted out of its original position many times. If the treasure were contained in wooden chests these have almost certainly rotted away by now, scattering their contents through the mud.

At least six people have died attempting to solve the Oak Island mystery. The expeditions

have cost far more than any treasure the pit may contain. And it is more than likely that no treasure will ever be recovered.

Almost as intriguing as the mystery of what is buried on Oak Island is the question of who buried it there. The Money Pit is far too complex a construction to have been made by a group of pirates. One suggestion is that it was built in 1780 by British army engineers. The British knew they were losing the American Revolution and they may have tried to hide the supply of money that was used to pay the army. This is an interesting theory; unfortunately, there are no records to indicate that it is true.

The Oak Island mystery remains as unsolved as it was when young Daniel McGinnis first stumbled upon it.

Knights in shining armor around the Round Table; the towers of Camelot; sorcery and swords—that's the world we think of when we picture King Arthur. Well, the truth is most of those stories are myths: the Arthur of the Middle Ages never really existed. But there was a real leader who lived centuries before, who may have been the model for the Arthur of legend. There was a real Camelot, too. We can't be sure about the Round Table.

In documents dating from the 7th century there are references to someone who may have been Arthur. Around the beginning of the 9th century a monk named Nennius put together a "History of the Britons." It was compiled,

Nennius said, from much older works. It clearly mentions King Arthur for the first time, and many of the later writings about Arthur are based on this historical document.

After the 12th century there was a flood of stories, poems, and songs about Arthur, not only from Britain but from France and other parts of Europe as well. There was something about the Arthur story that had enormous appeal. Arthur was a just and wise king and a victorious war leader who protected his people from wild and violent invaders. He was brought down, not by enemies on the battlefield but by treachery within his own court and family. The place of his burial was secret. Later writers were not interested in historical fact. They wanted to tell a good story, and they filled in this simple outline with all manner of miraculous events. They also gave Arthur and his knights the appearance and outlook of idealized heroes of their own time.

The most famous of the Arthur stories were written during the Middle Ages; that's why we think of Arthur as coming from that time. Today, most scholars believe that the historical King Arthur lived in the late 5th century. It was a time when the Britons, who had absorbed a

good deal of Roman civilization and were Christians, were being overrun by the invading Saxons, who were both barbarians and pagans. It was the period known as the Dark Ages. Traditions would have been passed on by word of mouth and were only written down at a much later time.

Arthur was probably a war leader, though not a king, who roused the spirits of his badly defeated countrymen and won a series of im- pressive victories over the  Saxons. His success may have been due to his knowledge of the Roman arts of war. He would not have worn a suit of armor, as metal plate armor was not worn at that time. At best, Arthur and his men would have had an iron cap and a shirt of iron links, or chain mail. Arthur is not a common name and may have been a Welsh form of the Roman name Artorius. In the 5th century many Britons still used Roman names.

Arthur would have faced overwhelming odds in battle, and so when he was killed, his followers may have tried to keep his death a secret so as not to encourage his enemies. This may have been the origin of the legend that Arthur is only "sleeping." Ultimately the Britons were overrun but they kept the tradition of their hero alive so that he would become an inspiration for later generations.

Many archaeologists now believe that Camelot was located at a place now called Cadbury Hill. This spot had been used as a fortress since the Stone Age, and was heavily fortified during Arthur's time.

Cadbury Hill is also near Glastonbury Abbey, which, according to tradition, is the place where Arthur was secretly buried. The tomb of King Arthur and his queen was supposedly located at Glastonbury in the 12th century. Arthur's tomb, however, is probably a hoax created by the Glastonbury monks who were trying to raise money to restore their abbey after a fire.

Wherever the king is buried, and whoever he really was, the legend of Arthur and his world lives on.

❖ *Burning People* ❖

On the morning of July 2, 1951 Mrs. Pansy Carpenter of St. Petersburg, Florida smelled smoke coming from the room of her lodger, 77-year-old Mary Reeser. With the aid of two men who had been working nearby, she broke down the door and was met by a blast of hot air. At first there seemed to be no sign of a fire. Then one of the men saw a charred circle where Mrs. Reeser's armchair had once been. Inside the circle was a heap of ashes, a few springs from the chair, a charred skull, and some pieces of human backbone. The most gruesome discovery was a foot in a black satin slipper; it was all that was left of Mrs. Reeser's body.

Can someone suddenly burst into flames and

burn up while his or her surroundings are untouched? Some people believe it does happen. The phenomenon is known as "spontaneous human combustion" (SHC). In the 19th century, it was thought that victims were alcoholics whose liquor-soaked bodies became so flammable that they ignited, "punishing" them for drinking too much. Episodes of SHC can be found in novels by Mark Twain, Herman Melville, and, most famously, Charles Dickens. In Dickens's novel *Bleak House*, published in 1852, drunken old Mr. Krook is reduced to a pile of ashes.

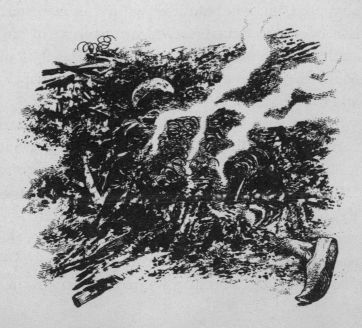

By Dickens's time scientists were convinced that SHC was a myth. Scientifically minded people assumed the author put the burning scene in his novel just for dramatic effect. But he didn't: Dickens really believed it could happen. When the author was criticized, he defended himself by writing a long essay on the subject in which he told of a large number of cases where people had apparently been suddenly burned up. Many of the author's friends and admirers were surprised and puzzled by just how passionately he held this belief.

You might think that no one believes in SHC any more, but you would be wrong. In fact there has been a serious revival of interest in the subject. Twentieth-century cases, like that of Mrs. Reeser, have been dug out of newspapers and the records of fire departments.

Most scientists think spontaneous human combustion is impossible. They say that what looks like SHC usually results when someone falls asleep while smoking a cigarette. Mrs. Reeser, for example, was a heavy smoker. If a person is sitting in an overstuffed armchair as she was, or lying in bed, the fire may smolder rather than flame up, and only a limited area will burn.

But such ordinary explanations don't satisfy everyone. The old theory that heavy drinking caused people to catch fire has been ruled out, but there is speculation that some sort of "natural electricity" builds up in the bodies of certain individuals and will, under special circumstances, cause them to catch fire. Most scientists, though, are completely baffled, and no one has yet come up with a convincing answer to the mystery of flames that appear from nowhere.

✤ *Creations of the Dark* ✤

The big mystery of the 1980s was crop circles. Areas of flattened wheat or corn that were usually circular in shape began appearing overnight in the fields of British farmers. No one ever saw who or what made them. Corn and wheat are easily crushed but there was no evidence of anyone or anything leaving a trail from the outside edge to the center. The British scientist Lord Zuckerman called the circles "creations of the dark."

There had been scattered reports of similar phenomena before. In the 17th century there were stories of the "mowing devil": circular patches of crops were mowed down and people thought some sort of diabolical creature was to blame. In the United States there had been "UFO nests": circular patches of flattened grass or scorched earth where a round flying saucer was believed to have landed. There were also reports of crop circles in Australia, Germany, and Japan. But the phenomenon remained mostly a modern British one.

The number of crop circles seemed to increase year by year, and their shape became more elaborate and exotic. Sometimes there would be a string of connected circles, or circles within circles. There were noncircular patterns including one which seemed to spell out the message WEARENOTALONE.

A whole network of individuals interested in the crop circle mystery developed. They were known as "crop watchers." Groups would spend night after night in fields that they believed were likely spots for new circles to appear. As interest in the mystery grew, the crop watchers were often joined by television crews and other journalists. No one ever actually saw a crop circle being formed.

There were many reports that strange lights in the sky—indicating the presence of UFOs— were often seen before the circles appeared.

Some people said that they felt sick after entering a crop circle. Crop watchers equipped with a variety of electrical measuring devices said that they could detect subtle electrical charges in the area of a crop circle.

As the number of crop circles grew, so did the number of theories to explain them. The most popular was that they were somehow connected with UFOs. Some theories revolved around whirlwinds or some other unusual but entirely natural phenomenon. Another suggestion, perhaps not a serious one, was that the flattened areas of grain were made by troops of badgers madly running around in circles.

Skeptics insisted that the crop circles were all a hoax. Flattening areas of grain is not all that difficult, they said, the key is not getting caught. While everyone was willing to admit that there were some hoaxes, many of those fascinated by the mystery insisted that it would have been impossible to fake many of the circles.

In September 1991 two retired artists, Doug Bower and Dave Chorley, said that they had been creating crop circles in southern England since 1979—when the phenomenon began. Earlier, a well-known crop watcher had stated that one of

Bower and Chorley's creations had to be genuine because it could not have been made by any human activity. When confronted with the truth he declared, "We have all been conned."

But this well-publicized confession did not end the crop circle controversy. The two men could not possibly have created all of the hundreds of crop circles. On some nights circles have appeared in fields hundreds of miles from one another. Are there a large number of other hoaxers involved, or is something else going on? Something strange and as yet unexplainable?

Will we ever know the answer?